MEATS
and Meat Dishes
Cook Books by Good Books

Phyllis Pellman Good • Rachel Thomas Pellman

Good Books

Intercourse, PA 17534
800/762-7171
www.GoodBks.com

MEATS
and Meat Dishes

Cook Books by Good Books

This is hearty food. Its source is the farm. Traditionally many families have raised their own steers, hogs, and chickens. So fresh meat is at hand. These dishes are

basic – not highly seasoned, not difficult to prepare. Natural flavors are allowed to shine through; nothing is wasted. And simple ingenuity makes all of it tasty!

Cover art and design by Cheryl A. Benner.
Design and art in body by Craig N. Heisey; Calligraphy by Gayle Smoker.
This special edition is an adaptation of *Meats: From Amish and Mennonite Kitchens, Pennsylvania Dutch Cookbooks.* Copyright © 1982, 1991 by Good Books, Intercourse, PA 17534. ISBN: 1-56148-037-1. All rights reserved. Printed in the United States of America.

Contents

Chicken Pot Pie

1 3½-4 lb. chicken   Makes 8-10 servings
1 cup celery, chopped
pinch saffron
salt and pepper to taste

1. Cook chicken and celery in 2 quarts of water until chicken is tender.
2. Remove meat from bones and set aside.
3. Add water to broth to make 3½ quarts, (several chicken bouillon cubes may be added to strengthen the broth).
4. Bring broth to boil. Drop pot pie squares into boiling broth and cook until tender. Return chicken to broth. Serve piping hot.

Pot Pie Dough

5 eggs
½ cup water
2¾ - 3¼ cups flour

1. Combine eggs and water and beat well.
2. Gradually add flour until soft dough is formed.
3. Cut into 3 parts. Roll each part on a cloth, rolling as thin as possible, using an additional 1 cup of flour to flour cloth

and dough so it handles well.
4. Cut into 1 inch squares with pastry wheel and drop into boiling broth.

Variation:
    Add 5 sliced, cooked potatoes to pot pie.

Creamed Chicken

2 Tbsp. butter or   Makes 4-6 servings
   chicken fat
2 Tbsp. flour
½ tsp. salt
dash of pepper
1 tsp. minced celery leaves
1 cup milk
1 cup chicken broth
2 cups cooked, diced chicken

1. Melt butter. Add flour, salt, pepper, and celery leaves. Stir until smooth.
2. Add milk and chicken broth. Bring to a boil and boil 5 minutes, stirring constantly.
3. Add chicken and heat thoroughly.
4. Serve with floating islands.

Floating Islands

    4 cups flour
    5 egg yolks
    12 Tbsp. margarine or butter
    milk

1. Cut together flour, egg yolks, and margarine to form coarse crumbs.
2. Add milk enough to moisten so dough can be rolled.
3. Roll dough thinly on floured surface. Cut into 1" squares or diamond shapes. Place on cookie sheet and bake at 350° until browned. You will need to watch these closely as some will finish baking before other.
4. Place islands in serving dish and cover with chunky chicken pieces and creamy broth.

    Creamed chicken may also be served over hot biscuits or waffles.

Chicken Croquettes

2 cups cooked chicken,   Makes 4 servings
 ground or chopped fine
pinch of celery salt
1 tsp. lemon juice
⅛ tsp. paprika
1 Tbsp. parsley
¼ tsp. chopped onion
1 cup white sauce

White Sauce

1 Tbsp. butter or margarine
1 Tbsp. flour
½ tsp. salt
⅛ tsp. pepper
1 cup milk

1. Melt butter; then add flour, salt, and pepper and mix well. Gradually add milk, stirring constantly until thickened.
2. Combine chicken, seasonings, and white sauce. Shape into croquettes and roll in bread crumbs. Then roll croquettes in beaten egg and again in bread crumbs.
3. Fry in deep fat for four minutes.

Chicken Pie

1 4 lb. chicken	Makes 4-6 servings

1 4 lb. chicken
1 bay leaf
2 stems celery, finely chopped
1 onion, thinly sliced
3 cups potatoes, cooked and diced
2 cups carrots, cooked and diced
1 cup peas, cooked
2 Tbsp. margarine or butter
2 Tbsp. flour
1 tsp. salt
⅛ tsp. pepper
1 cup milk
2 cups chicken broth
½ tsp. worcestershire sauce

1. Cook chicken with bay leaf until chicken is tender. Discard bay leaf. Remove meat from bones. Reserve chicken broth.
2. Combine vegetables and chicken and pour into casserole.
3. Melt margarine. Stir in flour, salt, and pepper. Gradually add milk and chicken broth. Stir in worcestershire sauce. Pour over vegetable/chicken mixture.
4. Cover casserole with pie crust.
5. Bake at 425° for 35 minutes. Reduce

oven temperature to warm and allow to set for 15-20 minutes. This helps to blend the flavors.

Pie Crust
   1 cup flour
   ½ tsp. salt
   ⅓ cup shortening
   3 Tbsp. cold water

1. Combine flour and salt. Cut in shortening till fine crumbs are formed.
2. Add water, 1 Tbsp. at a time and toss until all particles of flour have been dampened. Work mixture into a ball. Roll out and put on top of vegetables.

"Especially good on a cold day."

Chicken Roast

    3 whole chickens
    6½ quarts bread crumbs
    ½ lb. margarine
    3 cups chopped celery
    1 cup chopped onion
    6 eggs beaten
    ½ lb. margarine, melted
    2 tsp. parsley flakes
    6 tsp. salt
    1 tsp. celery salt
    1 tsp. garlic or onion salt
    1 tsp. paprika
    1 tsp. pepper
    3 tsp. poultry seasoning

1. Cook chickens till tender. Debone chicken and reserve broth.
2. Brown bread crumbs in ½ lb. margarine, stirring constantly.
3. Combine bread crumbs and all other ingredients except chicken. Mix well and add chicken broth till mixture is very moist.
4. Put chicken meat in bottom of a large roast pan. Cover with bread mixture.

5. Roast in a slow oven till golden brown (250° for 1½ - 2 hours).

"The traditional Amish wedding dish."

Baked Chicken

Dip chicken pieces in evaporated milk and then in cornflake crumbs. Arrange in single layer in roast pan or casserole. Cover. Bake at 350° for 1½ hours or at 200° while at church on Sunday morning.

Beef Roast

3-4 lb. beef roast   Makes 6 servings
2 tsp. salt
¾ tsp. pepper
¾ cup water

1. Rub meat with salt and pepper. Place roast in roasting pan.
2. Add 1 cup water. Cover and bake at 325° for 1½ hours.
3. Remove lid and bake an additional ½ hour to allow meat to brown.

Beef Gravy

3 cups water
2 Tbsp. flour
1 cup water
salt and pepper to taste

1. Add 3 cups water to browned beef drippings. Bring mixture to boil on top of the stove.
2. Make a smooth paste with the flour and 1 cup water.
3. Add paste to boiling drippings and water in a thin stream. Stir quickly and

constantly to prevent lumps. Add seasonings. Heat until thickened.
4. Serve with sliced beef roast and mashed potatoes.

Poor Man's Steak

2 lbs. ground beef
1 cup cracker crumbs
1 cup milk
1 tsp. salt
¼ tsp. pepper
1 onion, chopped

Makes 4 servings

1. Mix all ingredients together. Pat mixture out to ½" thickness on paper lined cookie sheets. Cover and refrigerate overnight.
2. Cut meat into serving size pieces. Coat with flour. Brown pieces in small amount of hot fat. Place in roasting pan and cover with mushroom sauce mixed with 1¼ cup water.
3. Bake, covered, at 300° for 1½ hours.

Mushroom Sauce

- 3 Tbsp. margarine
- ¼ cup mushrooms, chopped
- 1 Tbsp. minced onion
- 3 Tbsp. flour
- ¼ tsp. salt
- dash pepper
- 1 cup milk

1. Melt margarine. Add mushrooms and onion and sauté till tender. Add flour, salt, and pepper and stir until bubbly.
2. Gradually add milk, stirring constantly. Cook and stir until thickened.

Meat Loaf

- 1 egg   Makes 4-6 servings
- ¾ cup quick oats or bread crumbs
- 1 cup tomato juice
- ½ onion, minced
- 1 Tbsp. soy sauce
- 1 tsp. salt
- ¼ tsp. pepper
- 1½ lb. ground beef

1.   Beat egg. Add remaining ingredients and mix well. Form into a loaf and bake at 350° for 1 hour.

Variation:
Baked meat loaf may be placed on oven proof platter and frosted with mashed potatoes. Return to oven until potatoes are golden brown.

Sauce for Meat Loaf or Ham Loaf
   2 Tbsp. honey
   1 Tbsp. catsup
   1 tsp. lemon juice

Combine and use to baste meat loaf or ham loaf.

"A nice moist loaf that stays together."

Ham Loaf

1 lb. lean pork   Makes 6-8 servings
1 lb. smoked ham
1 lb. ground beef
1 cup milk
1½ tsp. salt
1 cup bread crumbs
2 eggs

1. Combine all ingredients and mix well.
2. Turn into roasting pan and shape into a loaf. Bake at 350° for 1½ hours.
3. Pour sauce over ham loaf and bake an additional ½ hour.

Brown Sugar Sauce for Meat or Ham Loaf

¾ cup brown sugar
1 tsp. mustard
½ tsp. paprika
¼ cup vinegar

Combine all ingredients and mix well.

Variations:
1. Add 4 oz. crushed pineapples to sauce.
2. Use 1¼ cup cornflakes crumbs instead of bread crumbs.
3. Add 1 lb. grated swiss cheese to meat mixture.

Snitz and Knepp

1 ham hock   Makes about 4 servings
1½ cups dried apples
2 Tbsp. brown sugar

1. Place ham hock in heavy saucepan. Cover with 2 quarts of water and boil 2 hours.
2. Add apples and brown sugar. Add an additional 1½ quarts of water and cook until apples are soft. Add knepp.

Knepp

2 cups flour
3 tsp. baking powder
½ tsp. salt
1 egg, beaten
2 Tbsp. melted butter
⅓-½ cup milk

1. Mix flour, baking powder, and salt. Add beaten egg, butter, and milk. Use only enough milk to make a sticky dough that will drop easily off a spoon.
2. Drop by spoonfuls into boiling ham and apple mixture. Cover tightly and boil for 15 minutes. Do not peek.

Baked Pork and Sauerkraut

1 pork roast   Makes 4 to 6 servings
27 oz. sauerkraut
3 cups water

1. Place pork roast in center of roast pan. Arrange sauerkraut around meat. Pour water over all.
2. Bake, covered, at 325° for 2½ - 3 hours, depending on the size of the pork roast. Add more water if sauerkraut dries during baking.

     This is a delicious cold weather dish. Serve it straight from the roast pan with mounds of mashed potatoes and home canned applesauce.

Baked Pork Chops

     Place 6 pork chops in bottom of shallow baking dish. Sprinkle with salt. Bake at 350° for 15 minutes. Cover each chop with bread filling and place 2-3 Tbsp. applesauce on top of filling. Return to oven and bake 1 hour longer.

Scrapple

1 lb. pork pudding meat   Makes 3-4 lbs.
1 qt. water or pork broth   of scrapple
salt and pepper to taste
1½ cups corn meal
¼ cup buckwheat flour

1. Stir pudding meat into 1 quart seasoned rapidly boiling water or pork broth.
2. When the mixture reaches the boiling point slowly add the corn meal and buckwheat flour. Stir constantly until thickened.
3. Cover and let simmer for 15 minutes over low heat.
4. Pour into two 1-lb. loaf pans. Cool thoroughly; then refrigerate promptly.
5. When scrapple is set, cut in ⅜ to ½ inch slices and fry in hot, greased skillet. When slices are browned and crusty, turn and brown on other side.
6. Serve hot with catsup, syrup, or apple butter.

"A hearty and traditional breakfast dish!"

Pig Stomach

1 large, well cleaned   Makes 4 servings
  pig stomach
1½ lbs. bulk sausage meat
6 medium potatoes, peeled and diced
1 small onion, chopped

1. Cook potatoes and onion together until potatoes are tender. Separate sausage meat into small pieces and add to potato mixture. Stir and cook only until sausage loses its reddish color.

2. Drain off excess liquid. Stuff mixture loosely into stomach and close all openings with skewers laced with string. Place in roast pan with ½ cup water. Place remaining mixture that will not fit in stomach in a buttered casserole.

3. Cover roast pan containing the stomach and bake at 350° for 2–2½ hours. After first hour prick stomach with sharp fork. Place casserole of remaining mixture in oven, uncovered and bake only for the last 40–45 minutes of baking time.

Overstuffing the stomach may cause it to burst while baking because the stomach shrinks considerably.

Variations:
1. Mix sweet potatoes with white potatoes.
2. Add 2 cups uncooked lima beans to stuffing.
3. Add 1 cup chopped carrots to stuffing.
4. Add 1 stalk chopped celery to stuffing.
5. Add ½ loaf of cubed bread to stuffing.
6. Add 1½-2 cups chopped cabbage to stuffing.

"We always called it 'Hog Maul'. We like to eat it at special times – Christmas or New Years or birthdays."

Sweet and Sour Sausage Balls

1 lb. sausage meat   Makes 5-6 servings
½ cup bread crumbs or cracker crumbs
1 egg, slightly beaten

Mix together. Form into small balls and brown.

Sauce

¾ cup catsup
⅛ cup white vinegar
⅛ cup soy sauce
¼ cup brown sugar

1. Mix together. Pour over browned sausage balls and simmer for 30 minutes.
2. Add water as needed during simmering to keep mixture from getting too dry.
3. Serve with rice or noodles.

"It's a lively way to serve sausage. The sweet and sour flavor is a favorite of ours!"

Barbecued Meat Balls

1 lb. ground beef   Makes 6 meatballs
1 egg
1 cup cracker crumbs
1 tsp. salt
¼ tsp. pepper
1 Tbsp. finely chopped onion
3 Tbsp. brown sugar
¼ cup catsup
⅛ tsp. nutmeg
1 tsp. dry mustard

1. Combine meat, egg, ¾ cup crumbs, salt, pepper, and onion. Mix well.
2. Mix together sugar, catsup, nutmeg, and mustard. Add half of this sauce to meat mixture. Mix well. Shape meat mixture into 6 balls and place in 3" muffin cups. Top balls with remaining sauce. Sprinkle with remaing crumbs.
3. Bake at 400° for 30 minutes.

"Very good. I will add this to my list of favorites for quick preparation and short baking time."

Barbecued Hamburger

2 lb. hamburger   *Makes 8 servings*
2 onions, chopped finely
½ cup catsup
1 cup tomato juice
6 Tbsp. brown sugar
6 Tbsp. apple cider vinegar
6 tsp. worcestershire sauce
6 tsp. prepared mustard

1. Brown hamburger and onion together.
2. Add remaining ingredients and simmer slowly for 45 minutes.
3. Pile into hamburger rolls to serve.

Turkey Barbecue

¼ cup butter or   *Makes 6-8 servings*
        margarine
½ cup onion, chopped
1 cup celery, chopped
¼ cup green pepper, chopped
¾ cup catsup
1 tsp. salt
2 Tbsp. brown sugar
1½ tsp. chili powder

1 Tbsp. worcestershire sauce
dash pepper
4 cups chopped, cooked turkey

1. Cook onion, celery, and pepper in butter until soft.
2. Add remaining ingredients except turkey and cook 5 minutes.
3. Add turkey. Heat thoroughly.

Tuna Burgers

1 7oz. can tuna fish   Makes 6 sandwiches
1 small onion, minced
¼ cup mayonaise
½ cup diced or grated cheese
1 cup chopped celery
6 hamburger rolls

1. Combine all ingredients for filling. Salt and pepper to taste.
2. Butter inside of rolls. Fill rolls and wrap in foil.
3. Bake at 350° for 20 minutes.

Fried Oysters

12 large oysters   Makes 12 oysters
2 eggs
2 Tbsp. milk
1-1½ cup cracker crumbs

1. Beat eggs and milk lightly.
2. Dip oysters first in egg mixture and then into cracker crumbs. Repeat this process once or twice to coat oysters.
3. Fry in deep fat until golden brown.

Scalloped Oysters

4 cups crackers,   Makes 4 to 5 servings
   coarsely crushed
1 10 oz. can medium sized oysters
2 cups milk
1 egg
1 tsp. salt
pepper to taste
⅓ cup butter or margarine

1. Line 1½ quart casserole with half of the crackers. Place half of the oysters on crushed crackers. Layer remaining crackers on top of oysters followed by the rest of the oysters.

2. Beat egg and add milk, salt, and pepper to it.
3. Just before baking pour mixture over oysters and crackers. Arrange butter in thin slices on top.
4. Bake at 375° for 30 minutes.

Deviled Clams

1 dozen large clams   Makes 12 clams
½ cup cold water
3 hard boiled eggs, chopped
onion and parsley to taste
bread crumbs
salt and pepper

1. Scrub clams well. Steam open. Save clam shells.
2. Grind clams. Add water, eggs, onion, and parsley. Thicken mixture with bread crumbs and season with salt and pepper. Form balls and pack mixture into half of the clam shells. Gently lower filled shell into hot oil and fry until golden brown. Clams may be fried ahead of time and kept warm in the oven.

Salmon Croquettes

2 cups flaked salmon   Makes 8 croquettes
4 Tbsp. flour
1 egg
2 Tbsp. minced onion
1 tsp. salt
1 cup bread crumbs
½ cup milk

1. Combine all ingredients and mix well.
2. Fry in hot oil in heavy skillet till browned on both sides.

Beef Tongue

1 fresh beef tongue
⅔ cup salt
⅓ cup brown sugar
pinch pepper

1. Mix salt, sugar, and pepper. Rub salt mixture into tongue. Place in airtight container in cool place for 3 days. Turn daily.

2. On the 4th day remove and rinse well. Cook about 2 hours or until tender. Cool 10 minutes. Peel outer skin from tongue.
3. Cool and slice.

Sour Gravy

2 cups cooked, cut-up roast beef   Makes 2-4 servings
2 cups water
⅓ cup sugar
2 Tbsp. vinegar
3 Tbsp. flour

1. Combine beef, water, sugar, and vinegar. Bring mixture to a boil.
2. Mix flour with enough water to make a smooth, thin paste. Gradually stir into beef mixture and cook until thickened.

"Delicious served on fried mush, stewed crackers, or old-fashioned baked egg omelet."

Liver Patties

1 lb. liver
2 slices bacon
1 small onion
1 egg, beaten
2 Tbsp. flour
1 tsp. salt
⅛ tsp. pepper

1. Grind liver, bacon, and onion in meat grinder or chop very fine.
2. Add beaten egg, flour, salt, and pepper and mix well.
3. Drop mixture by spoonfuls onto greased griddle or skillet.
4. Fry just a few minutes on each side.

"Left over patties make good sandwiches."

Barbecued Liver

Makes 4 servings

½ cup tomato juice
¼ cup water
2 Tbsp. apple cider vinegar
2 Tbsp. catsup
1 Tbsp. worcestershire sauce
1 Tbsp. brown sugar
½ tsp. salt
½ tsp. dry mustard
⅛ tsp. chili powder
2 Tbsp. bacon drippings
1 lb. beef liver

1. Combine first nine ingredients in small saucepan. Simmer for 15 minutes, stirring occasionally
2. Remove any veins or skin from liver. Cut into ½ inch strips.
3. Heat bacon drippings in large skillet. Add liver strips, stirring constantly over high heat, just until the meat looses its red color. Overcooking liver makes it tough.
4. Stir the barbecue sauce into the skillet containing the liver. Simmer together only until piping hot.
5. Serve over rice or noodles.

Creamed Dried Beef

4 Tbsp. butter   Makes 4 servings
¼ lb. dried beef, thinly sliced
½ cup water
4 Tbsp. flour
2½ cups milk

1. Brown butter in heavy skillet. Add shredded pieces of dried beef. Brown slightly. Add water and boil until water is evaporated. This helps to make the beef tender.
2. Sprinkle flour over beef and allow to brown slightly.
3. Slowly add milk and cook over low heat, stirring constantly. Cook until smooth and thickened.
4. Serve over baked potatoes or toast.

"A quickie meal – and substantial. The meat is so flavorful you only need a little bit to serve a bunch!"